Lightning
Beneath the Sea

I Haf ac Alaw

Megis morfil

Grahame Davies

Lightning Beneath the Sea

SEREN

Seren is the book imprint of
Poetry Wales Press Ltd.
57 Nolton Street, Bridgend, Wales, CF31 3AE
01656 663018
www.serenbooks.com
Facebook: facebook.com/SerenBooks
Twitter: @SerenBooks

The right of Grahame Davies to be identified as
the author of this work has been asserted in accordance
with the Copyright, Designs and Patents Act, 1988.

ISBN: 978-1-85411-575-1

A CIP record for this title is available from the British Library.

The publisher acknowledges the financial assistance of the Welsh Books Council.

Cover image: Anna Betts www.annabetts.com.

Printed in Bembo by Berforts Group, Stevenage.

Contents

The Hunt

New Bedford, Massachusetts

They still go out from here, the fishermen,
although you have to search these days to find
their rust-stained craft among the pleasure-yachts,
the pristine, white vacation voyagers.
They go with gasoline, of course, not sail,
not stars and sextants now, but satellites,
yet still the circling stormfronts when they stray
and still the waves' cold welcome when they fall.
That much has stayed the same since Melville's day:
out on *Acushnet* from New Bedford port,
back two years older, and a whaling man,
scarred, crown to sole, like Ahab, by the hunt,
ashore again, but not on solid ground.
Because it's always there, the enemy,
the one you would give everything to kill,
the one you cannot bear to live without,
greater than you are, guessed at, never grasped,
something with teeth, your lances in its side,
hidden in darkness, whiter than the snow,
silver in shadow, lightning in the sea.

Shoreline, New England.

This is the place the sea-road has to stop:
a circle of bare earth between the dunes,
the place you have to turn your car around
and take the pot-holed track the way you came.
We find a patch of verge just wide enough
to park the rental car, and leave it there,
hearing the sea now, as we close the doors,
and look round for a pathway to the waves.
We take a narrow track towards the shore
between the reed beds and the marram grass,
not thinking much, not really needing to,
drawn by the ocean's vast imperative,
the great sea that turns thoughts to grains of sand.
And isn't that the reason that we come,
when reason fails? To face an element
we cannot live in, and to feel alive?
To know that land, and life, must have an end,
and then return to them with gratitude?
Something like that, perhaps. But all I know
is that, when questions come, you'll find me here.

Two tyre tracks stretch before us through the sand:
some driver who thought walking to the sea
was something other people do. The path
curves round a final sandbank, and it's there:
a showroom four-by-four stuck axle-deep
in sand and water, and the hazards on.
There's someone sitting in the driver's seat:
a lady with big hair, her large-ringed hand
set lightly on the open window sill.
She lets the door swing out as we approach.
"Have you guys got a tow bar on your car?"
The voice is deep. She leans out. She's a man.
In lipstick, wig, mascara, but a man.
"I can't walk far in these, you see," he says,
and gestures to his sandals: strappy, gold,

and scarcely made for driving, let alone
slogging through sand dunes in a pencil skirt.
We shake our heads. We're sorry. Rental cars
don't come with tow bars. Can we phone for help?
"No need," he says. "I've called out the garage.
They'll bring the tow truck. I'll just wait right here."
We ask him if there's anything he needs.
"Nothing at all. But thank you all the same."
He smiles and sits back, waiting. We walk on.

When we come back, an hour or so has gone.
And so has he. The tyre-tracks in the sand
are doubled all along the narrow path,
where rescuers in oily overalls
had dragged him backwards to the asphalt road.

I think about him as I close our door,
and put the gearshift into drive. His smile,
his patient, unembarrassed waiting there
for help from strangers. Something in the way
he simply didn't mind uncertainty.
The shoreline's fading in the rear-view now.
I couldn't help him. But he did help me.

Cromer Pier

The crowds are out today. The carpark full,
queues at the chipshops, throngs along the rail
outside the Hotel de Paris to watch
the waiters' race, the runners spilling beer.
The winner gets a six-pack and a kiss
from young Miss Cromer, in her princess frock,
pulling her sash straight for the camera.
Behind them, on the pier, the fishers fish,
the walkers walk, the ice-cream vendors vend.
And all is as it should be, and has been
a century and more since engineers
pitched out this frail, gratuitous promontary,
this bridge to nowhere between sea and sky.

Down at the eastward end, a silver dome,
a theatre held at arm's length from the shore
as though to prove a point – that shows go on,
perhaps, that songs are stronger than the storm,
that art can stand against an angry sea.
The kind of strutting, wanton showmanship
that builds a monastery on a mountaintop
and dares both hell and heaven to come and see.

Next to the theatre, another hall,
the lifeboat station, whose proscenium arch
is open to the weather and the waves,
the shifting stage whose audience is the air.
The lifeboat, balanced on the slipway, waits,
like one of those collection box displays;
the single penny of a stranger's soul,
will send it, calm, where God would fear to go.

A summer Sunday. On the promenade,
the old recall their childhood holidays,
and find the town grown smaller with the years.

The young, whose only scale is sea and sand,
think nothing ever changes. In the fair,
the carousel's stiff, painted cavalry
revolve to music never heard elsewhere,
and pennies rattle in the dark arcade.

The nearness to the edge, the nothingness
that makes all things that live seem more alive,
perhaps that's why we come. Perhaps that's why
we set this cast-iron causeway in the sea,
as far as we can get from solid ground,
to hold the stage and slipway side by side,
as close to the horizon as can be.

Islanders

The island. Population twenty-three,
and never to climb back to twenty-four.
The future that they planned will never be,
and emigrants don't come here any more.

So isolated, one lifetime ago,
the world had been at war more than a year
and no-one even thought to let them know,
or take their one slow-smiling volunteer.

An only son. A boy with film-star looks,
though no-one on the island thought that way,
a place where scarcely anyone had books,
and films were rumoured things from far away.

He went, survived, came back to work the land,
his generation older every spring.
Their children, few and lonely, could not stand
the emptiness that swallowed everything.
They left the past surrounded by the sea.
More houses now than people. Let it be.

Pendine Portents

Being all the warning signs at Pendine Sands, Carmarthenshire

No boats.
No metal detectors.
No unauthorised motor vehicles.
No unauthorised vehicular access.
Vehicles must not be parked on the concrete.
or on the road leading up to it.
There are large areas of sand unsafe for vehicles.

There is no lifeguard service operating.
Beware of tides.
Beware of motorised craft in the boating lane.
Beware land sailing.
Beware of rip-currents near the cliffs.
Beware personal water craft.
Unusual objects on the beach must not be touched.

Do not litter.
Do not swim in boating lane
or near cliffs.
Do not use inflatables when windy.

Persons using the beach do so entirely at their own risk.
Danger of explosions.
Danger of death.

CCTV is in operation.
Clean up after your dog.

Discovery

It's down a sidestreet,
not so far you can't still hear the traffic,
but unfrequented all the same.
One of those bookshops
with shelves out on the pavement
for books not worth the stealing
you can browse while passing by.

And it's there I find it,
after so many years,
so many sidestreets,
so long that I can hardly credit now it's real,
real as its leather binding
and the few traces of gold leaf
left in its tooling,
so many pairs of hands it has been through.

The price? That's immaterial:
for this one volume
it would be worth the sale of all you have,
buying the shop,
the street,
worth everything.

And yet it's here, now, in my hand,
heavy with answers,
asking only the one cold coin
of my belief.

Capital Bookshop, Cardiff

A battered volume that's seen better days
and on the flyleaf, in a careful hand:
"Dear John brought this the night he left Cathays."

It's Belloc's verse. Who reads him, nowadays?
Small wonder it's for sale, here, secondhand,
a battered volume that's seen better days.

There's more than love and leaving in that phrase;
a circumstance I don't quite understand:
"Dear John brought this the night he left Cathays."

The *night* he left. A parting of the ways
at evening time. Precipitate or planned?
A battered volume that's seen better days.

A goodbye stiff with silence and clichés?
And more than friendship when he took her hand?
"Dear John brought this the night he left Cathays."

A long-dead love; no record of it stays
except, on this old bookstall's bargain stand,
a battered volume that's seen better days
"Dear John brought this the night he left Cathays."

Dangerous

I found it lying in the bargain box
with hopeful horoscopes for years gone by
and annuals for single-series shows
and guides to countries that have changed their names,
the *ne plus ultra* of the printed word,
the last ledge before landfill or the fire.
The Dangerous Book for Boys. I snatched it up,
as though there had been other browsers near
ready to claim it if I didn't act
decisively. *The Dangerous Book for Boys.*
Living a bit too dangerously, it seemed,
but rescued now, and coming home with me.
The star maps – that was why I wanted it.
I should explain: these last few autumn months,
the evenings drawing in, I've felt the need
to know the names of stars. Nothing too hard,
nothing too specialist, only the names
of those unjoined dot puzzles in the sky,
the famous ones, the ones you ought to know.
And here they are: two pages, all I need.
Two circles to enclose infinity
and show its suburbs like a railway map.
The price? I check the title page. A pound.
For all those stars, a steal. I wonder why
its owner let it go? His writing's here,
big bold and confident. A generous man.
I'm no graphologist – I don't need to be –
the words speak for themselves: "To my dear son
Now our adventure's over, in the faith
you'll find success in study and in life,
because they are the self-same joyous thing."
Outside the autumn evening's drawing in.
Too early yet for stars, but when night comes
I'll use this book to find some pattern there,
or try to. What was it the father said?
Studies and life – the self-same joyous thing.

Final Page

She closed her book with tenderness and care,
the girl beside me on the bus, and then
she stroked the pages like a lover's hair.

A student by her clothes – that studied air
of nonchalance I noticed in her when
she closed her book with tenderness and care.

What final words had she been reading there,
what author gifted beyond tongues of men?
She stroked the pages like a lover's hair.

An old and battered book whose spine is bare,
Some childhood friend she reads, then reads again?
She closed the book with tenderness and care.

Or finished for the first time? A voyeur,
I wish I knew what prayer brought this amen.
She stroked the pages like a lover's hair.

But, smiling to herself, she's unaware,
held by the power of that unknown pen.
She closed her book with tenderness and care;
she stroked the pages like a lover's hair.

Errata

My Life and Loves, Volume II, Frank Harris, 1925

p8   'youg' for young
p15   'inconccivably' for inconceivably
p30   'Bessy' for Bessie
p76   'honseless' ought to be houseless
p127 'overton' ought to be 'Ovington'
p179 Homosexualist, not homsexualist
p279 Delete comma after 'maiden'
p298 'Tock' should be took
p356 'Drived' should be drivel
p358 'Bushed' should be hushed
p373 'Nuissances' should be nuisances
p377 'Deadfully' should be dreadfully
p394 A colon after 'twitched' should be a comma
p412 'Temtation' should be temptation

Charity Shop

It's not the kind of volume that I buy,
the glossy, tasteless, coffee-table kind;
small text, big pictures, easy on the eye:
Unlock the Secrets of Your Dreaming Mind.
The sort of book you buy to give away.
And yet, perhaps there's more here than there seems –
the inside cover's been inscribed this way:
"Dear Bea, come home and we can share our dreams."
Her parents' names, her sister's, and the date
– God help them – scarcely 18 months ago:
their tripped, dream-chasing daughter didn't wait
before she let this hopeful hardback go.
I buy the unread, two-pound-fifty tome
to give, if not the child, the book, a home.

Reader

She's there each morning as I walk to work
along the blind arcade of terraced streets.
When almost every other curtained bay
is still drawn close to keep the morning out,
her window, always, is a square of light.
And in the bottom of the frame, her shape,
back to the window, showing nothing more
than dark curls and a hand that holds a book –
all you can see above the sofa back.
The walls are almost bare: an abstract print,
a wide-screen television, never on:
this house's one apparent tenant needs
no entertainment but her library.
And needs no job as far as I can see,
if she can spend the whole day reading there.
I turn the corner, and she turns the page.

And every afternoon, and every night,
when I come home, diminished by the day,
I see her there, her hand and head unmoved:
a good three hundred pages, I would guess,
she gets through every day. I envy her:
her solitude, her lust for literature,
her single room that overflows with time,
her days spent doing what she loves to do.
I never see her face. Her age, her looks,
are always unrevealed. But all the same
she fascinates me – all those hours she spends
with nothing more than words. What she must know.
What she could talk about – and listen to.
Better, of course, that we should never meet,
never be disappointed. After all,
is that not why we read: to spend our days
with paper, not with people? People fail.
The only true perfection is the page.
Written, or read. No company compares.
We keep our back towards life's window, while
we use its light to read our stories by.
Her open curtains let the last light fall
golden across the page. The shadows climb.
She lifts the book a little, and reads on.

Building Work

It's gone, that sixties office block
with metal window frames,
yellow and flaking.
Gone too, the TV showroom,
redbrick, glass-fronted,
and all its shining screens I used to lipread
while waiting for the school bus home.

And the kebab house,
its full-wall menu glowing red and gold.
And the taxi office, its fag-end-cratered floor,
its vinyl sofa split and spilling foam.

Only a month or so I've been away,
and now the whole block's gapped,
more space than structure now,
the great part razed, reduced to level ground.

Only the creative has been kept:
that Georgian double-front;
those Gothic window-arches,
with weathered sandstone carvings,
that smooth, stone-panelled, art deco facade.

I stop the car to watch.
A lorry's leaving, laden with debris;
a banksman stops the traffic, waves it out.
A dumper driver waits his signal to reverse;
the banksman stands, hands off the holding traffic,
waves him through the chain-link fence, and turns.

She's young,
her hair under the yellow helmet tomboy short.
In steel-toed boots, in grey-green overalls, in charge.

She lets the stream of traffic flow again,
and walks away, into the empty site,
where the concrete foundations
are already sending up their rigid metal shoots.

Remembrance of Things Past

For Marcel Proust, remembrance of things past
was brought back by a simple madeleine,
and with its taste he left the world of time
with crumbs of childhood in his lap again.

For me, it's not a biscuit with my tea
that brings remembrance, as for M'sieur Proust,
but a bacon sandwich with tomato sauce
as breakfast in a cafe in Llanrwst.

We'd start our work at six to load the van
with hot bread from the ovens before dawn,
then drive it out through freezing country lanes,
the load of bread behind to keep us warm.

And after making sure the valley farms
and pubs had got their rations for the day,
we'd stop at ten for bacon sandwiches
and mugs of tea to keep the cold away.

And when I taste a bacon sandwich now,
lost times come back to me, like M'sieur Proust,
and I'm fifteen, it's cold, but I can smell
the bacon in a cafe in Llanrwst.

Quarry

One day every year, they say,
it takes delivery.
Of what, no-one knows,
except that it needs guards and guns.
Which day, no one knows.
Only that it is never the same day.

Walkers come, diverted to this crushed-slate path
by rumour,
stop where the path must stop at the metal gate,
not high, no Berlin wall,
but barbed-wired, enough.
They peer through, rattle the padlock – it's new –
look round, get bored, move on.

Probably, the secret is – there is no secret.
Beyond the gate only the forests,
growing someone's profit decades hence,
the path ending in some sterile clearing.

A half dozen times, perhaps, I've been there,
on aimless Sundays, or with visitors
needing a story.
Always the same half-hope, the half-hour vigil,
until the weight of silence drives you home.

It was the same today.
But as we walked away, we heard a drag of metal,
and turned to see the gate wide open,
a squaddie to one side, just pocketing the key.

And then, ahead, an engine's sudden growl,
and past us it came, smaller than I'd imagined,
but here: a tractor with two tankers,
going too fast for us to see the labels.
Were there labels?

The driver was in army gear. And young.
And as I fumbled with my camera phone,
the gate had closed behind them and they'd gone.

Compatriot

Llangollen International Eisteddfod

Every year they came, the travelling tribes:
Australians so tall our Celt-sized beds
could not contain their southern hemisphere frames;
Soviets who, delivered to the decadent Dee valley,
mysteriously lacked the roubles to fly home;
Zulus who, to thank our village for its welcome,
danced bare-breasted outside the parish hall,
so that even the statue on the war memorial,
its eyes downcast in municipal mourning,
couldn't help but stare.

Every year we went,
since I was boot-high to a Cossack,
glad to swap a day at school
for this rainbow rendezvous in the Berwyn hills,
to collect the autographs of Scots or Magyars,
and have our pictures taken with white-kimonoed girls,
never thinking for a moment it was strange
that every summer the nations should gather
beneath World's End,
in freedom, fellowship, and fancy dress.

Every year, still, I go,
as much for the memory as the moment.
And even though the journey now
is many miles from Llan,
many years from then,
somehow I need to see it all the more,
this one-week vision of a world made right.
And if you've watched the things you've cherished die,
or seen what hate can do, or bitterness,
violence or unforgiveness, you'll know why.

Grey

I think that all the lasting things are grey:
the clouds above the mountains when it's late.
When all around you changes, these things stay.

The lichen where the quarry works decay,
the tides that fill the harbours in the strait.
I think that all the lasting things are grey.

The twilight in the cwm at close of day,
the ash the coalfire leaves within the grate.
When all around you changes, these things stay.

The mist that hides the slagheaps' scars away,
the winter rain that shines upon the slate.
I think that all the lasting things are grey.

The seagulls wheeling over Cardiff Bay,
the patient sea that bore a nation's freight,
When all around you changes, these things stay.

The home we build with steel and stone today,
and blend our light and darkness to create.
I think that all the lasting things are grey.
When all around you changes, these things stay.

Valley Villanelle

I see that it's to journey that we go;
I'm starting to discern the spirit's way,
I see it's only faith if you don't know.

The daily comradeship of men brought low,
the dole-queue jokes while waiting for your pay,
I see that it's to journey that we go.

The jobless kids who help the language grow,
the Valleys voting 'Yes' to have their say,
I see it's only faith if you don't know.

A walk up to the mountain for a blow:
the mother takes the baby out to play;
I see that it's to journey that we go.

I see, through grief, the grace that lies below,
and how, to live, you give your life away;
I see it's only faith if you don't know.

The burning blessing when the answer's no;
the stinging balm of silence when I pray.
I see that it's to journey that we go.
I see it's only faith if you don't know.

The Mountains

Your silence angered me,
meeting my questions with a stony face,
remaining impassive before my pain.
The emptiness of the sky,
the coolness of the wind across the moor,
the indiscriminate heather scents,
and, like an angry son, I cursed your stark indifference.

Now, when I come to you,
carrying my cares to the high country like sacrifices,
my breath shorter, the path more rocky,
it is your very silence that I seek:
the quiet counsel of the mist among the ferns,
the wordless empathy of the earth's touch,
and I appreciate, now, the wise restraint
that keeps its silence before man's complaint.

Transmitter Stations

These places always fascinated me:
always on hilltops, always kept secure
by barbed wire fences, locks and warning signs,
to keep the world away, while they transmit,
twenty-four-seven, one-way monologues.
Amid the beauty, far from beautiful,
blocks of no-nonsense brick utility.
Imagine what it must be like to work
in one of these. The gate locked shut behind,
the solitude – not loneliness – the shifts,
the cups of tea to mark the passing hours;
inside, electric warmth, outside, the wind.
And all the time, sending your message out.
Ideal, really, when you think of it.

Rough Guide

It happens inevitably,
like water finding its level:
every time I open a travel book,
I sail past the capital cities, the sights,
and dive straight into the backstreets of the index
to find that in France, I'm Breton;
in New Zealand, Maori;
in the U.S.A. – depending on which part –
I'm Navajo, Cajun, or black.

I'm the Wandering Welshman.
I'm Jewish everywhere.
Except, of course, in Israel.
There, I'm Palestinian.

It's some kind of a complex, I know,
that makes me pick this scab on my psyche.
I wonder sometimes what it would be like
to go to these places
and just enjoy.

No, as I wander the continents of the guidebooks,
whatever chapter may be my destination,
the question's always the same when I arrive:
"Nice city. Now where's the ghetto?"

The Complete Index of Welsh Emotions

Being all the directions in the Welsh and English Hymns and Anthems, published by The Welsh National Gymanfa Ganu Association Inc. 1979.

Stately
With dignity
With dignity, much feeling
With deep feeling
With feeling and dignity
Dignified, reverently

Jubilant
Jubilant style
In jubilant style
In singing style
Dedicative style

Majestic marked rhythm
With marked rhythm
In stately rhythm
Steady martial rhythm
With flowing rhythm
Flowing rhythm earnestly

Majestically
Triumphantly
Meditatively
Prayerfully
Brightly with confidence

Joyously
With joy
Joyous and majestic
Steady, joyous

Not too fast, with joy
Not too fast, expressive
Not too fast, with feeling
Not too fast, with sincerity
Not too fast, with solemnity
Not too slow, meditatively
Not too slow, jubilant

Moderate
Moderate with feeling
Moderate with deep feeling
Moderate with much feeling
Moderate with conviction
Moderate, with much expression
Moderate, reverence
Moderate, with reverence
Moderate, with great reverence
Moderate with spirit
Moderate, spirit of joy
Moderate, flowing rhythm
Moderate, with serenity

Moderate, sweetly
Moderate, thoughtfully
Moderate, prayerfully
Moderate, broadly

Moderate, expressive
Moderate, dignified

Moderately fast
Moderately fast, brightly
Moderately fast, joyfully
Moderately and rhythmically
Moderately slow, with reverence

With reverence
With reverence
With great reverence
With fervour
With spirit
Spirit of praise
With breadth and earnestness
With exaltation
With feeling – andante
Andante con dolore
Broadly with exaltation.

Sweet Peas

Bought in Vermont, planted in Wales.

"If they've not come by now, they never will."
The dozen seed pots in their plastic tray
are undisturbed by any touch of green,
although I planted them two months ago
in early March. And now it's early May.
   "This spring's been cold. Perhaps a few more days..."
   "It's not the season, it's the seeds themselves.
   They must be dead, or they'd be up by now."
She puts the tray back on the greenhouse shelf
where other soil-filled cells have split with life
striving towards the sunlight.
   "It's a shame,"
I said, remembering how, six months ago,
I'd paid two dollars fifty for that pack,
imagining the way, once they were grown,
I'd say: "Oh, those. I grew them from some seeds
I got from Robert Frost's house in Vermont.
His son would sell sweet peas to travellers
for pocket money. And they grow there still.
They're gorgeous, aren't they?" Or, invited out,
by writers, I would bring some with the wine,
so that their scent and colour might suggest
good taste on all our parts, especially mine.
We'd put them loosely in the vase, as though
the musk we all remember, and the smooth
irregular unfolding of their leaves
were unremarkable, at least to us.
   "Maybe they just don't travel very well.
   Perhaps the earth is colder over here."
She doesn't answer. On the greenhouse door,
the paint has blistered in last summer's sun.
   "You're sure they're dead?"
   "As sure as I can be. ·
   But there's no need to take my word for it.
   We'll leave them here, and if they come, they come."
A cloud has stepped between us and the light.
We close the door to keep the warmth inside.
   "Another week, perhaps..."
   "Perhaps," she says.

The Dark Forest

The Hunter

It would have been so easy –
snap the eye of conscience shut: an oubliette,
show the knife a moment's light,
the blood's sudden smile, the head wilting like a snowdrop.

In the entrails of the forest, no need to smother her scream,
she was already disappeared,
a rootless refugee, no parents to grieve,
the perfect private prey,
sealed in a lead coffin in some cellar of my mind
with the royal warrant's red wax upon the door.

To execute the little traitress, such a simple task.

But as I faced her on the clearing,
with only the trees to tell,
I knew we shared a single soul,
our silent roots touching underground.
And as I set her free, I freed my own heart too.

I slaughtered my servility like a pig.
That night, I knelt before my queen,
offering, guiltless, my gilded trophy:
the bloodstained box which held the secret
of my scarlet sedition.

Revisiting

It's twenty years exactly since I last
walked down these college corridors to class;
now, on a weekend visit to my past,
the lobby's new, the polished floor like glass.

And quiet too. But no surprise in that;
only the keenest would be here today
in study cubicles where I once sat,
a rainy Saturday in early May.

Businesslike, clean; no posters on the door,
no student scruffiness, except a trail
along the whole length of the gleaming floor:
the muddy footprints of a barefoot girl.

Along the passageway where I once went
to lectures, she came splashing from the street.
What panic, pain or pleasure could have sent
her through the mud with nothing on her feet?

But at the far end of the passageway,
a girl's belongings in a hasty pile –
a sign: "Hamlet auditions here today" –
her overcoat, her unlaced boots, her file.

The marks our lives make never really go.
The tracks she left behind as she passed through
the corridor I walked, decades ago,
are transient as mine were, and as true.

Nothing is lost. I close the door, walk on.
She came, unshod, through dirty city rain,
to show the present and the past are one,
long-drowned Ophelia, alive again.

O Beata Trinitas

Three sights I recall:
sun on the grass,
shade in the hall,
and the clouds over the moor.

Three sounds I know well:
the seagull's cry,
the chapel bell,
and the friend's voice at the door.

Three scents that remain,
an open book,
earth after rain,
and the south wind from the shore.

Berries

The fallen leaves lie deeper every day.
The branches grow more bare; the seasons turn.
Beside the path, the sea-cliff falls away;
the webs are threads of winter through the fern.
Behind the rusting fence, a bunch or two
of blackberries the birds have left behind,
forgotten in the briars as they grew;
the season can turn cold, but still be kind.
They let themselves be lifted from the stem
more freely than perhaps I thought they would,
as though the threat of frost had readied them
to stain warm fingertips, as berries should.
I spit the seeds out, hard and dark and live:
the bitter juice that lets the thorn-tree thrive.

Weather Forecast

The stalls in the market at Pontypridd are loaded up heavy with gear,
and the men in the pubs down in Pontypridd are loaded up heavy with
      beer,
and this Christmas Eve in Pontypridd is the coldest day of the year.
And that was the subject of one exchange I happened to overhear:
"I don't think it's cold enough to freeze." "Now, I'm telling you so you
      know –
if anything falls from that sky tonight, it'll fall in the form of snow."

The kids are tired and shouting, and their mams are worn to rags,
struggling to bring tomorrow home in fifteen plastic bags,
the wrapping paper, kitchen foil and bargain Christmas tags,
and Bristol Cream and Carling and two hundred king size fags.
The clouds are grey above the terrace roofs where electric Santas glow.
And if anything falls from that sky tonight, it'll fall in the form of snow.

The pavements are strewn with nightclub flyers and ads for Bargain
      Booze,
the kind that only those in the lowest income brackets use,
the arms that hold the collection buckets are patterned with tattoos;
because no-one's more generous than those with little left to lose.
The sky is as dark as it must have been two thousand years ago.
And if anything falls from that sky tonight, it'll fall in the form of snow.

I've left the valleys where people shout their greetings in the street,
where people will use your Christian name the first time that you meet,
the towns whose men make men the whole world over seem effete,
and no-one will let you get away with snobbery or conceit.
But no matter far I've travelled, no matter how far I go,
whenever the cold is biting deep and the heavy clouds are low,
I recall those words I overheard, and I smile because I know:
if anything falls from that sky tonight, it'll fall in the form of snow.

Midwinter

No breezes move the branches; no birds sing;
December's frost has turned the world to grey.
The earth in winter trusting for the spring.

The silver hedges where the dead leaves cling;
the clouds that shroud the winter sun away.
No breezes move the branches; no birds sing;

The bitter cold that makes your fingers sting,
forms icy mist from anything you say.
The earth in winter trusting for the spring;

No life, no movement now in anything;
no difference between dawn and dusk and day.
No breezes move the branches; no birds sing;

The solstice of the year, when everything
is balanced between increase and decay.
The earth in winter trusting for the spring;

No sign of what another day may bring;
the seeds of hope are frozen in the clay.
No breezes move the branches; no birds sing.
The earth in winter trusting for the spring.

Disillusion

Never to trust again,
not a priest, not a politician,
not a mentor, not an author,
not a lover, not a friend.
And not myself,
certainly not myself.

Never to give again,
not my money, unquestioning,
not my hope, undoubting,
not my time, unstinting.
And not my love,
no, certainly not my love.

Because they all fail;
dream more than they can do,
promise more than they can be,
believe that they are better than they are.
We all do.
And what is best of us
dissolves like incense in a chancel.

And now, knowing this,
expecting nothing,
wanting nothing,
fearing nothing,
to trust, to give, to love.

Prayer

Spirit, use me today,
not in some miracle
that would make others marvel
and would make me proud.

Not in the word of wisdom
that would stay in the mind
and make me always remembered.

Not in the heroic act
that would change the world for the better
and me for the worse.

But in the mundane miracles
of honesty and truth
that keep the sky from falling.

In the unremembered quiet words
that keep a soul on the path.

And in the unnoticed acts
that keep the world moving
slowly closer to the light.

Propempticon

Wind from the east where day is breaking,
take this prayer to the western sea.
Find her sleeping or find her waking,
but find her, wind, for me.

Touch that face that I cannot look on,
the cheek that I touched long ago,
but softly, so that she does not waken,
gently, so that she does not know.

Give her the blessing that I would give her
if she were still at home with me,
and let her think it is just the weather
over the western sea.

Crossroads

It was at the junction there with Palace Road,
the rush-hour traffic queueing at the lights,
that our paths crossed one evening in the dusk,
I walking tired from my office work,
and she, red tracksuit, hair tied quickly back,
rushing, it seemed, towards, or from, the gym.

A good friend's daughter, I'd known her as a child,
turning cartwheels on the carpet in our home,
at five or six. And now, past college age,
and taller, by some way it seemed, than me.

She stopped, surprised, a little out of breath,
and laughing at our sudden meeting there,
and at our newly re-adjusted heights.

Yes, she said, she'd done her first degree,
but now, a music postgrad for a while,
she balanced work and studies, fees and friends,
and violin, and sport, and bars and beers,
and travelling to Thailand. Like you do.
At least if you are smart, and twenty two.

And me? Well, thanks for asking, much the same.
I mean... not bars and backpacks, but the same
I was before. Just that much older now.
Wiser? Well, that's not for me to say.
Working of course. There isn't much choice there,
what with the kids, the mortgage, college fees...
But writing? Yes, stilll writing, thank the Lord.
The one thing keeps me sane. It's just the time,
or lack of it. I wish I could do more.
But there are always bills you need to pay.

She nodded, understood, or thought she did.
I told her I should really let her go.
I saw that she was rushing when we met.
Yes, she said, just running to the shop,
then back for my next client on the hour.
Her client?

    Yes, she said. A prostitute
can't keep them waiting for her on the street.
It's all about discretion, as you know.

I didn't know. She saw I didn't know,
and gently smiled at my astonishment.
It's just to pay the college fees, she said.
It's just a job like any other one.
You trade some time and trouble for their cash,
and spend the surplus on what gives you joy.

Of course you do, I said. Of course you do.
But didn't mean it as I wished her well,
and watched her run towards the corner shop.

I walked on, wiser now, perhaps. Perhaps.
I thought of what she'd said. The time, the trade.
The guiltless freedom that her labour bought.
And walked on, wiser, yes. Of course you do.

Hoodie

We were walking past the cemetery –
the light had gone; the dark had not yet come –
when I saw him in the shadow to the left,
approaching us, his hoodie grey as ash.
I looked away, the way you learn to do:
eye-contact makes them plague you all the more.
Pretend you have not seen them and walk on.
Ignore the outstretched hand, the bitten nails,
the sharpened phrases that addiction hones
to slice between your conscience and your cash.
They never go away, are never homed,
employed or fed for all the coins you throw.
Only the hunger grows, the bitterness,
that you, presentable, are safe and seen.
He did not speak. I looked back. He was there,
a yard away, and shorter than I'd thought,
and younger too, his shadowed cheeks unlined,
but somehow not because he was not old,
but more as though he had been young too long:
like for a lifetime, for eternity.
I know the death, the knife under his cloak,
the knowledge that he carries like a blade.
He does not even need to look at me:
his grey mask does not smile and does not move.
Nor can I move, or look away, or run.
His hand comes up, as though on puppet strings,
and mine goes out and takes it, and we're one.

Margin

It was a long way down,
and even though the cliff curved, concave,
to the shore,
and even though the sea was calm,
and even though the offshore breeze behind me was light
I kept a careful distance from the edge.

Then he passed me, impassive,
a man like me, but naked,
a gold-framed portrait of a family
– his, surely –
held like a holy icon
to his chest.

And stepped out, unhesitating,
impatient, almost,
into the empty air.

I could not bear to look
where his body must be broken
somewhere between the breakers and the brink.

It was later I returned,
months later,
after a journey well-attained,
and this time, not alone,
but squired and sistered
by the one companion,
and this time, walking between the cliff-edge and the sea.

We found his falling place,
remembered,
knew we should not look.
But looked.

Naked still, and foetal,
and pillowed on his portrait, still intact,
but covered over with a patterned cloth
as though
a curtain had made shift to be a shroud.

I knew I should not touch.
But touched him, with my foot,
Gratuitously.

And then we ran,
ran as we had to do,
as he stirred,
stood,
and stumbled after us,
gathering pace.

We could not even spare the glance behind,
but raced, at the edge of breath,
across the slipping shale, the escarpment's shingle,
until, at last, the scrubby path,
the spaced steps downward,
roofs and trees
and solid shapes of society.

The attendant seemed to know us,
let us pass
with a smile that mixed acceptance with contempt,
showed us the way to safety.

We looked behind at last:
the pursuer was far off,
and walking away,
and clothed now.

We watched him go, and wondered why,
why did we have to run?

Messenger

He was running again,
the latest message racing in his head;
the third time today
on the same narrow track
between the gorse hedges,
between two masters,
with deadlines always shifting,
always more urgent.

At least, this time, it was downhill,
and fast.

Round that sharp corner, yet again,
and twenty yards ahead, it's blocked –
a bloody brand-new silver Merc coupé,
spotless, driverless,
the alarm light blinking slowly on the dash.

He didn't even break his stride –
bonnet, roof and boot: three steps,
light, not enough to dent the metal,
just to print it with the stain of earth,
then back, heavy, to the mud and stones,
and on,
leaving, on the showrooom silver,
three dark swastikas,
accidental, unmistakeable
from the worn pattern of the sole.

Goodbye

I told her and her friends they'd have to leave;
this was a home and not a boarding house,
and not a place for them to ply their trade.
Let them go rent their own place, and goodbye.
Not later. Now. Goodbye. And close the door.
I went to lie down as they got their stuff
using stage voices as they ran me down.
So disappointed – and I'd seemed so nice.
Wait till they told their friends about it all.
And then they came, unbidden, one by one
and placed, unasked, a dry kiss on my cheek.
She came the last of all, suitcase in hand,
months of reproaches packed into her eyes.
Told me I'm not the man she thought she knew.
And kissed my cheek. "I never was," I said.

Piano Solo

She took my hopes away in plastic bags,
not even bothering to wrap them first.
All my ambitions too she packed away
in cardboard boxes, none too carefully.
My pride, she left it out for passers-by
to ponder on the pavement in the rain.
And all my thoughts, each phrase and syllable,
in notebooks, theses, marginalia,
she took, until the house that we had shared
was cleansed of every crumb of sustenance
as though, at Pesach, of all leavened bread.
Only the upright piano stayed behind;
too heavy, with its solid iron frame,
to carry out, and not at concert pitch,
beyond all tuning, sticky in the keys,
its varnish scratched with now-grown children's names.
I play it, and the sound is sharper now
than when soft furnishings would deaden it.
It's clearer than before: the empty rooms
are, to these solo tunes, hospitable.
I play it badly, but I always did;
there never was a time I played it well.
These days I'm learning, not proficiency,
but not to mind if sometimes notes are wrong.
The playing is the purpose, and for that
better to have a broken instrument.
And silence is a better audience,
and solitude is better company,
and emptiness, I find, is all I need:
the dusty stripped-wood floorboards resonant,
sun through uncurtained windows on the keys.

Pathways

Taking the path to the dark hollow,
knowing there is a place
between the shadow and the dark.
Taking the track to the hill's edge,
knowing there is a place
between home and hiraeth.
Following the brook upstream,
knowing there is a place
between being and becoming.

★

Prayer for the Dying

When you have to leave,
do so like the raindrop from the cloud.
When you have to leave,
do so like the tide goes from the shore,
strong, knowing it is time.
When you have to leave,
do so like the falcon from the crag,
do so like the leaf from the ash tree
on a windless day.

★

Jacket

God, how I wanted to be just like him:
the looks, the learning, the leather jacket too.
I even bought one just like his
and wore it for a while. It didn't fit.
And I lost it, later, somewhere on the way.
Today, I met him, after all these years
unchanged. He carried something in his arms.
The jacket. "Here", he told me, "Put it on.
You see," he said. "Now you've grown into it."

Salvage

You made your mark here for a short while, true,
and then you went your way, as we must do,
but let us salvage these discarded things,
and keep them from oblivion – for you.

Infinity, the thickness of a hair,
the turning stars, the movement of a chair;
and every speck of dust contains it all,
no separation between here and there.

Departed

They touch our lives much less than we suppose,
the dead. The ones who swore they'd never leave,
but did so. Those who slipped away and those
we said we'd miss, but didn't really grieve.

The ones who, with their patience or their pain,
left us resolved we'd live a different way;
to never lie, or slander, or complain;
although we did so, almost the next day.

The great ones, even, known or by report,
whose spirits wrote in stars across the sky;
they count for little, or the truths they taught;
they bring us no new wisdom when they die.

We don't admit it, even when it's clear,
the way the least beloved human face
is more to us than those no longer here,
the ones we said no others could replace.

It's not the tragic, but the trivial things
that bury sadness deeper every day;
not how creation sighs, but how it sings,
though that itself is tragic, in a way.

The daily sunlight staring through the glass.
The portrait fading in the painted frame.
The wind that goes, ungrieving, through the grass.
The loved one's lonely, lichen-covered name.

Song for Samhain

The wall between the worlds grows thin
when darkness falls on Samhain night.
Open the door and let the dead come in.

Fine as the filigree which spiders spin
to hold the leaves of autumn in their flight,
the wall between the worlds grows thin.

Those who are safe past sanctity and sin,
those who have gone the dark road to the light.
Open the door and let the dead come in.

Wind at the keyhole; cold upon the skin;
shapes in the shadow, sheltered from the sight.
The wall between the worlds grows thin.

Love from our lost ones, kindness from our kin,
prayers that we pray, and blessings we recite,
open the door and let the dead come in.

Now let the season of the soul begin;
welcome the wanderers who return tonight.
The wall between the worlds grows thin.
Open the door and let the dead come in.

Taliesin

I met him at the bridge across the stream
down from the mountain. He's a mountain man.
The handrail was worn silver. You'd not dream
flesh could wear rust to silver. But it can.
We spoke about the music that he'd taught,
decades ago, when he and I were young.
The songs were always sad, but life has brought,
sorrows as sharp as any that were sung.
And as we talked, the river flowed away,
going where fallen leaves and sunlight go,
going no swifter now than yesterday;
there's nothing in this loss I didn't know.
He told me things I loved would never last.
They didn't. But I loved them as they passed.

Beltane Blackbird

I never thought to see so cold a May:
the slow insistent east wind every day,
makes fingers stiff as winter at their work,
and sunlight seems another world away.

You might have known it colder, years ago,
some faded snap of nineteen-sixties snow.
I could have turned to ask you as we talked –
it was the kind of thing you used to know.

The hardened soil is heavy on the spade,
the ice is still unmelted in the shade,
where every broken branch and blade of grass
the frost, like February, has fabergé'd.

No birds this morning on the fencing wire,
only a single blackbird on the briar:
the song you always said you waited for
will be for us, each May, a Beltane fire.

That unshared bottle of your best Bordeaux;
the things we should have said, and yet we know,
they do not matter now the blackbird sings:
welcome the green and let the winter go.

Passenger

It was so beautiful, the woman's voice,
that even in the rush-hour bus –
the carping car horns, mouthy mobile phones,
the tinny iPods' canned cacophanies –
it made me look up from my newspaper.
"Excuse me, please. I need to get off here."
A voice to open doors, to open hearts,
to make you love her just by hearing it.
She turned to thank the man who moved for her,
and as she did so, I could see her face.
Not like her voice. No, nothing like her voice.
Enormous, disproportionate and skewed
as though by mirrors in a fairground stall.
I recognised her from a TV show
about those who, by accident or birth,
have what they kindly called distinctive looks.
Some bone disorder. Some long Latin name.
There was an operation, so they said,
could make her go unnoticed. She refused,
was happy as she was. The shock, the stares
were other people's problems. She was fine
the way she'd always been, would always be:
spared superficiality each time
she met a stranger, always undeceived,
loved for herself, and – let me say it – loved,
for the uncovered soul that voice revealed,
that I remembered when she'd turned and gone
past the distorting mirror on the stair.

The Wellesian Brothers

They had some style, whoever built this place.
I'll say that for them. They had money too.
These marble floors, these pillars don't come cheap.
That desk there, where the priest is sitting now,
preoccupied, his Spencer Tracy head
bowed over papers, that must be antique.
That retro telephone? Original.
These paintings, well, look at the Vatican,
the wealth they have there. This is just the same.
Nothing too good for God. Something like that.
The one acknowledgement we've had so far
from Spencer is a frown. And so we wait.
Is it the way we're dressed? Is it the way
your arm slipped round my waist familiarly
as we sat down on this plush velvet couch,
which looks more comfortable than it feels?
He's going now: off down the corridor,
black brogues clicking on the shining stones.
A door creaks, closes quietly to itself.
And we're alone. On this side table here,
a spread of literature, like tarot cards:
postcard-sized tracts on everything from sin
to sanctity, and all points in between;
all design values decades out of date,
and moral values, centuries at least.
But in the centre, leather-bound in blue
a volume like a presentation book,
whose worth is more in what it cost to bind
than what is bound within it. Just for show.
The letters on the dark-blue hide are gold:
"Who Are These Brothers?" and the author's name.
Who were they? Something they no longer are.
That much seems certain. Something people saw
and spent hard cash to keep on doing good,
so they themselves could keep on as before.
Who were they? Men whose goodness turned to gold,
and sacrifice to silver. Alchemy.
The door creaks open. Footsteps on the stone.
There's still no smile. We know, some way, he's right.
But also know, in some way, so are we.

Plas Power

The grassy slopes have long been left behind,
the treeline too, the town-lights on the plain.
Only this hand-cut pathway through the rocks
shows there is any place for humans here.
The time it must have taken – years, perhaps –
to carve this out, those convict labourers,
and make it wide enough for carriages.
And all for what? Just so some millionaire
could say he had a mountain hideaway
and make his minions climb there, mile by mile
to pay him court. Victorian vanity.
And yet I'm climbing too, unwillingly.
One final corner round the mountainside,
and there it is, surrounded by the stones:
grey gables, towers, wrought-iron tracery,
like something Poe or de la Mare would build
if words were wealth and poems property.
The hallway light is on. I push the door
and get the welcome I had thought to find.
The stairs curve round like strands of DNA
past portraits of the saints with upcast eyes,
up to the first-floor landing, where she stands,
hands folded, face in shadow, dressed in black,
still as a sculptured Justice, and as cold.
This is where I should climb, obedient.
But something in her silence made me stop.
"Come down," I told her. "You come down to me."
She made no move, said nothing. "You come down."
I said again. The shadows on the stair
shrouded her face.
        Then she was coming down
slowly into the lamplight. "You." I said.
She took my hands just like when we were young
and led me down towards the silent hall.
The passing years have left no mark on her.
 "Wherever you go, I will go," she said.
The door before us opened on the night.
The host of saints behind us looked away.

I thought of all the years, the loneliness,
"Why did you stay here all this time?" I said.
Beyond the door, our pathway to the plain
lay twisted through the black and broken stone.
 "Don't you recall?" she said. "You put me there."

Doorway

I must have passed it by a thousand times,
this unmarked doorway off St Mary's Street,
next to the gents' outfitters and the bank.
Two thousand times, perhaps, and never guessed
what lay behind. I never noticed it.
Only today you said we should go in.
I followed you, expecting – I don't know –
some narrow stairway to the upper rooms:
small-time attorneys, one-man surgeries,
some private flats, perhaps. But never this:
this vaulted giant cavern of a hall.
Everyone's here. People I haven't seen
for decades, people that I thought I knew:
newspaper staff, and college lecturers,
and many more whose jobs I can't recall.
At work, some of them, on those banks of desks;
at lunch, those others on the farther side,
seated at canteen tables by the wall.
There must be hundreds here, and yet the space
is still too large. What did it used to be?
High by the moulded ceiling there's a name,
a faded trompe l'oeil: 'Palace of Joy.'
A music hall, then, one time, long ago,
and now turned into this compendious space,
for labour and for rest – for everything.
For music too: those couples over there
are charlestoning to jazz-age melodies,
in period costume, and with all the moves.
Where could they find time in a working day?
I would have stayed and watched, but you walked on
and started up the curving marble stair
that leads up to the wrought-iron galleries.
"Come on," you said, "there's plenty more to see."

Notes

(Capital Bookshop) Cathays (pronounced 'Cat-ays', with the accent on the second syllable), is a district of Cardiff.

(Errata) Harris (1856 –1931), was a hell-raising author, editor, journalist and self-publicist educated at Ruabon near Wrexham and best-known for his inventive erotic memoirs My Life and Loves, a succès de scandale of the 1920s. That book's errata are given here as a found poem in their entirety without omission or re-ordering.

(The Dark Forest) In the fairy story, the hunter disobeys the wicked queen's order to kill her stepdaughter Snow White and he presents the Queen with a pig's heart, saying it is the victim's. Translated from my Welsh in the summer school of the British Centre for Literary Trans-lation.

(O Beata Trinitas) Part of a larger work for choir and orchestra commissioned by the composer Karl Jenkins to mark the granting of university status to Trinity College, Carmarthen.

(Propempticon) A form of Greek verse to wish well to a friend departing on a journey.

(Salvage) Written to mark the exhibition 'Salvage' by sculptor Nigel Talbot, and in memory of the death of a friend of the artist.

Thanks and acknowledgements

My particular thanks go to Amy Wack for seeing potential in this volume, and for guiding it through the press; thanks also to Mick Felton, Simon Hicks and all at Seren for their customary hard work and dedication. I am grateful to Bob Holman, founder of the Bowery Poetry Club in New York City, for suggesting the title of this collection, and to Stephen Rees for preserving the Welsh folk-song from which the words, in translation, are adapted. In Wales, for fellowship and inspiration, my thanks go to fellow poets Peter Finch, Ifor Thomas and Morgan Francis, and all in the Vulcan Circle.

In America, for guidance, teaching, hospitality and friendship on my journeys, of all kinds, I am indebted, among others, to: Tom Cowan; Jack Maguire; Susan and Bill McClellan; Jane Vieira; Mark Woods; Gary Lindorff; Shirley Oskamp. Pam Myers, David Price, Karen Blomain, Michael Downend and Ed Moran. I am grateful to Anna Betts for the cover image, to Mick Gower at Anglia Ruskin University; to Angharad Wynne and Eric Maddern for friendship and for the hospitality of Cae Mabon where some of these poems were written. Thanks also for the hospitality of the Community of the Sacred Heart at Llannerchwen in Powys, and for the learning opportunities presented by the Hereford and Monmouthshire Jungians. I am glad to acknowledge the assistance of a bursary from Literature Wales, the national literature promotion agency, in buying time to work on the book.

I am grateful to the editors of the many journals and collections where some of these poems first appeared, or if translated from the Welsh, where they first appeared in English. 'Rough Guide' appeared first in *Poetry London* and has been much anthologised. 'Valley Villanelle' appeared first in *Oxygen* (ed. Amy Wack and Grahame Davies, Seren, 2000). 'Remembrance of Things Past', 'The Mountains', and 'Prayer' appeared first in *Ffiniau/Borders* (with Elin ap Hywel, Gomer, 2002). 'Revisiting' and 'Whitewash' all appeared first in *Poems of Love and Longing* (ed. Viv Sayer, Gomer, 2008); 'Margin', 'Building Work' and 'Propempticon' appeared first in *Kalliope*. 'Grey' appeared in *Villanelles* (ed. Annie Finch and Marie-Elizabeth Mali, Everyman, 2012).

'Grey' was commissioned for the laying of the foundation stone of the Wales Millennium Centre, and was later set to music by Karl Jenkins; 'Compatriot' is from a commission by HRH The Prince of Wales for Llangollen International Musical Eisteddfod. 'O Beata Trinitas' is from a commission by Karl Jenkins to mark the creation of Trinity St David's University at Carmarthen. ' 'The Dark Forest' was translated during a residency at the British Centre for Literary Translation's summer school at the University of East Anglia. 'Salvage' was requested by the artist Nigel Talbot to commemorate the death of a friend. 'Propempticon' was commissioned by the German literary magazine, *Kalliope*.

As always, my profoundest love and thanks go to Sally, Haf and Alaw. *Megis morfil.*

Also by Grahame Davies

non-fiction

The Dragon and the Crescent: Wales and Islam (Seren, 2011)

Real Wrexham (Seren, 2007) Reprinted 2009

The Chosen People: Wales and the Jews (Seren, 2002)

Sefyll yn y Bwlch (University of Wales Press, 1999)

fiction

Everything Must Change (Seren, 2007)

Rhaid i Bopeth Newid (Gomer, 2004)

poetry

Achos (Barddas, 2005)

Ffiniau/Borders (Gomer, 2002) With Elin ap Hywel

Cadwyni Rhyddid (Barddas, 2001).Reprinted 2002

Adennill Tir (Barddas, 1997)

anthologies

The Big Book of Cardiff, Eds. Peter Finch & Grahame Davies (Seren, 2005)

Gŵyl y Blaidd/Festival of the Wolf, Eds. Tom Cheesman, Grahame Davies and Sylvie Hoffman (Parthian/Hafan, 2006)[a]

Nel país de la borrina (VTP Editorial, 2004)

No país da brétema (VTP Editorial, 2004)

Oxygen, Eds. Amy Wack & Grahame Davies (Seren, 2000)